Reading Essentials® in Social Studies

COUNTRY CONNECTIONS II

AUSTRALIA

JOANNE MATTERN

Perfection Learning®

Editorial Director: Susan C. Thies

Editor: Mary L. Bush

Design Director: Randy Messer

Cover Design: Michael A. Aspengren

Inside Design: Michelle J. Glass, Mark Hagenberg

IMAGE CREDITS:

© Bettman/CORBIS: pp. 22, 33 (center); © Dave G. Houser: p. 27; © Michael & Patricia Fogden/CORBIS: p. 14; © Yann Arthus-Bertrand/CORBIS: p. 8 (center); Corbis Royalty-Free: pp. 7, 10; The Kobal Collection: pp. 33 (bottom), 40; © Elizabeth Watt Photography/Stockfood: p. 35; © Gary White Photography/Stockfood: p. 36

Corel: front cover, pp. 1, 2–3, 9 (bottom), 18 (top), 23; Clipart.com: pp. 5, 17 (bottom), 18 (bottom), 19, 21, 24, 31, 38; Comstock: p. 6; Library of Congress: p. 13 (bottom); Map Resources: pp. 4, 9 (top); Photos.com: back cover, pp. 8 (bottom), 13 (top, center), 15, 16, 17 (top), 18 (center), 20, 25, 26, 29, 32, 39, 42, 43

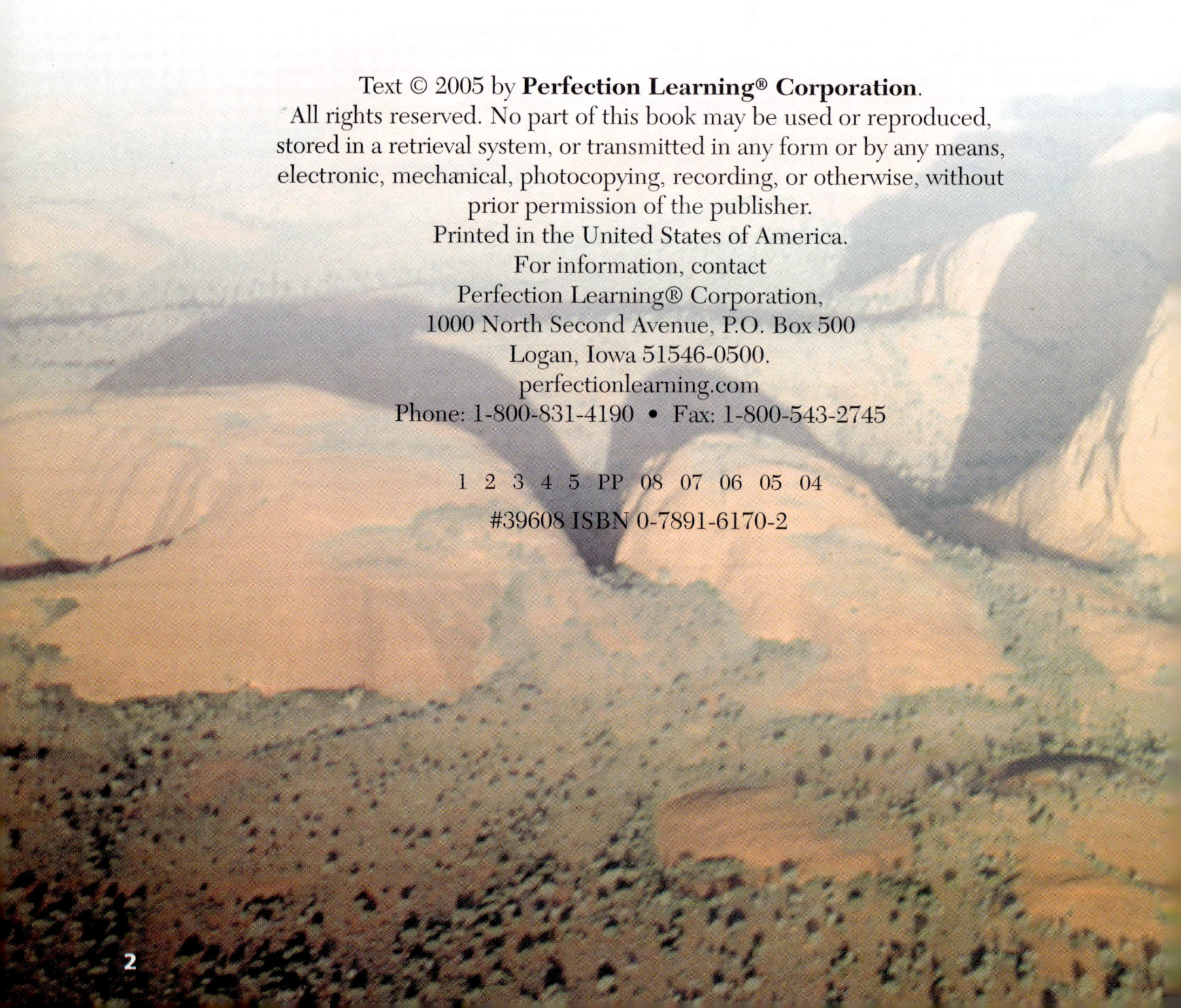

Printed in the United States of America.
For information, contact
Perfection Learning® Corporation,
1000 North Second Avenue, P.O. Box 500
Logan, Iowa 51546-0500.
perfectionlearning.com
Phone: 1-800-831-4190 • Fax: 1-800-543-2745

1 2 3 4 5 PP 08 07 06 05 04

#39608 ISBN 0-7891-6170-2

Melbourne

Geographical Features A large part of Australia is flat land. Most of the western and central parts of the country are covered by deserts and **plains**. Rain forests grow along the tropical northern coast. Mountains rise in the east. The country's main **river system** flows from the Great Dividing Range to the Indian Ocean. The Great Barrier Reef is located off the eastern coast of Australia.

Highest Elevation Mount Kosciuszko (7310 feet above sea level)

Lowest Elevation Lake Eyre (53 feet)

Climate The weather is temperate, or mild, in southern Australia. Central areas of the country are hot and dry. Northern Australia has a hot, humid climate.

Capital City Canberra

Largest Cities Sydney, Melbourne, Brisbane, Perth, Adelaide

Population 19,731,984 (2003)

Official Language English

Main Religion Christianity—Anglican (Church of England), Catholic, Methodist, Lutheran

Government Australia is part of the **British Commonwealth** but governs itself. A governor general represents the British king or queen. A prime minister is the head of the government. The laws are made by the **Parliament**. Australia is divided into six states and two **territories**.

Industries mining, industrial and transportation equipment, food processing, chemicals, steel

Natural Resources bauxite, coal, iron ore, copper, tin, gold, silver, uranium, nickel, lead, zinc, diamonds, natural gas, petroleum, sheep, cattle, poultry, wheat, barley, sugarcane, fruits

Currency basic unit is the Australian dollar

AREAS OF AUSTRALIA

The six states and two territories in Australia are Western Australia, South Australia, Queensland, New South Wales, Victoria, Tasmania, Northern Territory, and the Australian Capital Territory.

DOWN UNDER DOLLARS

One United States dollar is worth about one and a half Australian dollars. So for every kangaroo you can buy in the United States, you can buy one and a half kangaroos in Australia!

The Australian flag design includes the flag of England, a seven-pointed star representing the six states and the two territories combined, and the Southern Cross constellation.

CHAPTER 1

Beneath Your Feet

Australia's Land and Climate

Australia is the smallest continent on Earth. However, it is the sixth-largest country in the world. It may seem confusing that Australia is both a country and a continent. But the island is too large to be part of another continent and too small to be divided into lots of countries.

AN IMPRESSIVE ISLAND

At almost three million square miles, Australia is the largest island in the world.

The small island of Tasmania is considered part of Australia. At one time, Tasmania was attached to Australia. Then about 12,000 years ago, it became a separate island when the ocean rose over the land that connected the two areas.

DEVOURING DEVILS FROM TASMANIA

Remember the cartoon character Taz who races around in a whirl? He's modeled after real Tasmanian devils. These fascinating creatures are **native** to Tasmania. They will eat almost anything. Their powerful jaws and teeth devour all of their prey—even the fur and bones.

Despite their scary name, Tasmanian devils are very shy and usually run away from people. They got their name from the spooky whining sound they make when they're angry.

IN THE BEGINNING . . .

Millions of years ago, Australia was part of a supercontinent called Gondwana. Gondwana included most of the countries south of the equator. Over many years, Gondwana broke up into separate continents. After Australia broke away, the oceans became deeper. This cut off Australia from other landmasses, creating the island continent.

GEOGRAPHICAL FEATURES

Australia is one of the world's flattest places. The average **elevation** is only about 1000 feet above sea level.

About two-thirds of Australia is covered by hot, dry plains called the *outback*. This land is located in western and central Australia. The outback's harsh environment makes it a difficult place to live.

WHAT'S A BUNGLE BUNGLE?

It may sound like a Dr. Seuss character, but it's really a great geological structure found in Western Australia. The Bungle Bungle Range is a group of beehivelike mounds that have formed over millions of years. The Bungle Bungle has orange and black stripes of rock, mineral, and **algae**. It is surrounded by **gorges** and natural pools.

Bungle Bungle

Australian outback

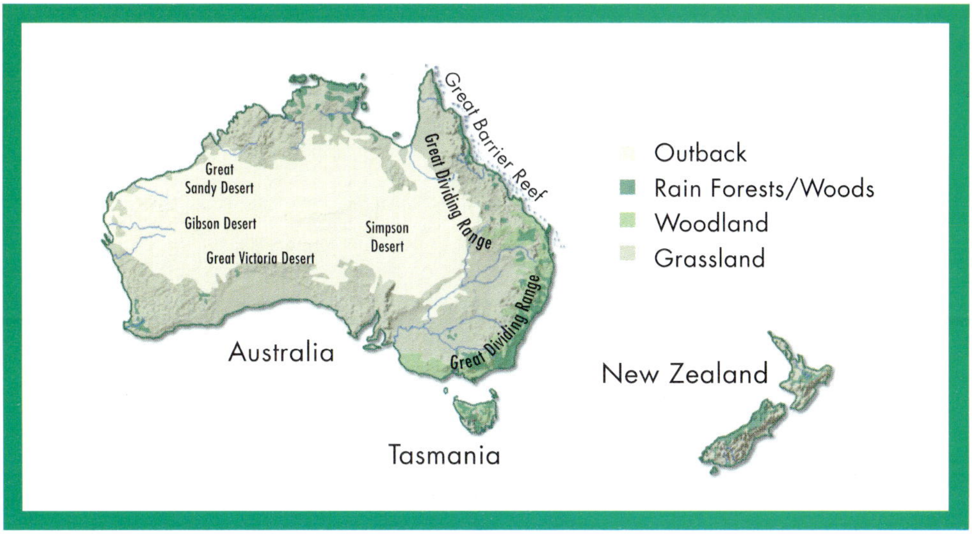

Much of the outback is desert land. The Great Victoria, Gibson, and Great Sandy Deserts lie on the western half of the outback. The Simpson Desert is located on the eastern half. All of the deserts except the Gibson are covered with sand and dunes. The Gibson Desert has a rocky surface of small stones and pebbles.

Other parts of the outback are known as "the bush." These areas are covered with **scrub** plants. These are plants that have **stunted** growth, in large part due to the hot, dry climate. Acacias, scrubby eucalyptus trees, and saltbush shrubs are common bush plants.

The coasts of Australia are very different from the hot, dry outback. The northern coast of Australia includes a warm, wet area of rain forest. Coastal plains spread across the eastern edge of the country. About 85 percent of Australia's people live on these coasts.

MONSTROUS MONOLITH

The outback is home to the world's largest monolith, or large rock structure. Ayers Rock rises in the middle of the outback. This enormous block of red sandstone is almost 6 miles around at its base and is 2844 feet high.

Ayers Rock is also known as *Uluru*. Uluru is the name that Australia's native people, the Aborigines, gave the rock long ago.

Great Barrier Reef

The Great Barrier Reef stretches for 1250 miles along the northeastern coast of Australia. This reef is the largest known coral formation in the world. Coral reefs are made from the skeletons of tiny animals called *polyps*. These polyps grow next to one another, forming a chain, or reef. Each polyp makes its own protective cup. After a polyp dies, its cup remains. These hard cups form the coral reefs. Fish and many other creatures live and feed in the waters around the Great Barrier Reef.

The eastern coastal plains are separated from the outback by mountains called the Great Dividing Range, or the Eastern Highlands. Most of these mountains are only about 4000 feet tall. That's less than a mile! The highest peak is Mount Kosciuszko, which is 7310 feet tall. The Great Dividing Range includes **plateaus**, gorges, and canyons.

Australia depends on its rivers to provide drinking water and water for crops. Many of Australia's rivers, however, are only full during the rainy season and are dry the rest of the year. Water from these rivers is stored for use during the dry season.

Two important rivers in Australia are the Darling and the Murray. The Darling River is the country's longest river. At more than 1700 miles, this river flows southward from the Great Dividing Range until it meets the Murray River. The Murray River and its **tributaries** flow west from the Great Dividing Range and eventually empty into the Indian Ocean. This river system covers more than 1600 miles.

THE CLIMATE

The climate varies in different parts of Australia. The outback is hot and dry. Average temperatures are about 85°F and can reach as high as 113°F. Parts of the outback receive less than 10 inches of rain each year.

The northern coast of Australia has a very different climate. This area is hot and humid and receives 60 to 100 inches of rain a year. Northern Australia has only two seasons—a hot, wet summer and a warm, dry winter.

Southern Australia has a temperate climate. It doesn't get really hot or really cold. Temperatures here average about 70°F in the summer and about 50°F in the winter. This area has four seasons with cool winters and warm summers.

During the summer, the southern part of Australia is exposed to hot, dry winds. These winds often cause severe **brush** fires. Southeastern Australia, including Tasmania, has some of the largest brush fires in the world. These fires destroy millions of acres of forest. They have also destroyed homes and other buildings in their path.

SEASONAL SWITCH

Because Australia is in the Southern Hemisphere, its seasons occur at different times than those of the countries in the Northern Hemisphere, such as the United States. When students in the United States are on summer vacation (June to September), Australian students are experiencing winter. Australians have summer fun in December through March. Autumn in Australia falls from March until June. Spring is from September to December.

CHAPTER 2

Living Wonders

The Plants and Animals of Australia

Because Australia is an island continent, it is home to many plants and animals found nowhere else in the world. These species were cut off from other continents when ocean levels rose millions of years ago. Animals that lived in other places had a difficult time **migrating** to Australia. This led to an unusual mix of wildlife in the country.

PLANTS

About 22,000 species of plants grow in Australia. Ninety percent of these plants are native to Australia. The other 2000 species were introduced, or brought, to Australia by settlers from other parts of the world.

The trees in Australia vary by location. Australia's coastal areas have many acres of **evergreen** forests. The northern rain forests include palms, ferns, vines, beeches, oaks, ashes, and cedars. Swamps filled with mangrove trees can also be found in the northern part of the continent.

Perhaps the most well-known Australian tree is the eucalyptus. Forests of these trees are found in southern Australia. The eucalyptus tree grows quickly and can stretch to a height of 300 feet. Puffy white flowers grow alongside narrow green leaves. The eucalyptus tree is a good source of lumber and oils that are used for perfumes and medicines.

A STEADY DIET

Eucalyptus leaves are the only food eaten by koalas. These animals have special pouches in their cheeks to store the leaves. They also have extra-long intestines to help digestion.

Another common plant in Australia is the acacia. Australia is home to more than 500 species of acacia. One type of acacia is the golden wattle. The flower's pleasant scent is used for perfumes. Its wood is used to make furniture. The golden wattle is the national flower of Australia.

COAT OF ACACIAS

A coat of arms is a symbol of a country. It is often used to represent a country during times of war. Australia's coat of arms is decorated with a background of wattles. It also features a kangaroo and an emu.

Australian coat of arms

Western Australia is home to many species of wildflowers. Between August and October, this area is carpeted with brilliant colors from a variety of flowers. One of these flowers is the kangaroo paw. This tube-shaped flower with a velvety surface is used for medicines by the Aborigines.

During the rainy season, the desert areas of the outback are covered with small trees, shrubs, and grasses. Many of these plants have roots that stretch deep beneath the ground to reach underground springs of water. This helps the plants survive in the hot, dry environment.

Desert pea

The desert pea is a flower that grows in western and southern Australia. The flowers of the desert pea are red with a black center. While able to grow in the dry outback, this plant especially thrives after heavy rains.

Animals graze on different grasses that grow in the outback. The most common is called *flinders grass*. This plant is found in Queensland and the northern part of New South Wales. It is a dry, scraggly plant with long, thin leaves. Flinders grass grows well in sandy clay soil.

ANIMALS

Marsupials The most unique animals in Australia are mammals called *marsupials*. Like other mammals, marsupials are **warm-blooded**, give birth to live young, and nurse their babies with milk. However, marsupial babies are not completely developed when they are born. Right after birth, they crawl into a pouch on their mother's stomach. The babies stay in this pouch for several weeks or months as they continue to grow. When they are fully developed, they come out of the pouch and begin life on their own.

Kangaroos are probably the most well-known marsupial around the world. These animals are champion jumpers. Their powerful back legs help them leap more than 30 feet in one jump. Kangaroos can run 40 miles per hour (mph) over short distances.

A joey in its mother's pouch

Kangaroo

Baby kangaroos are called *joeys*. Joeys are only about the size of a lima bean when they are born. They quickly crawl into their mother's pouch and live there for about six months. Even when a joey is old enough to live on its own, it will stick its head back into the pouch to nurse on its mother's milk. A joey will even climb back into the pouch when it's scared or just wants to be close to its mother.

LONELY MARSUPIAL

The North American opossum is the only marsupial found outside of Australia.

Wallabies are smaller members of the kangaroo family. About 50 different types of wallabies live in Australia. They make their homes in caves, cliffs, and rocks. Special pads of rough skin on their back feet help them hop around on the rocks.

Wallaby

Koala

Although they look like cuddly teddy bears, koalas are *not* bears. Koalas are marsupials that spend most of their time in trees, eating and sleeping. Their sharp, curved claws help them hang on to the branches. Light gray or brown woolly coats protect koalas from cold, rainy weather.

THIRSTY KOALAS

Koalas rarely drink water. They get most of their moisture from eucalyptus leaves. In fact, the word koala comes from an Aborigine word meaning "no drink."

Other Australian marsupials include wombats, cuscuses, numbats, bandicoots, sugar gliders, and marsupial moles and mice. Each of these animals is an interesting creature with its own special habits.

Other Mammals Australia is also home to many interesting nonmarsupial mammals, such as dingos, platypuses, and echidnas. The dingo is a wild dog that yelps or whines instead of barks. Dingos live and hunt together in groups called *packs*.

Dingo

Platypuses are strange-looking animals with webbed feet, "duck" beaks, and flat "beaver" tails. These creatures are the only mammals that have poisonous venom. They store this poison in spurs on the insides of their back legs and use it to protect themselves.

Echidnas look like porcupines. They are covered with long, sharp spikes. These mammals also resemble anteaters because they use sticky tongues to eat ants and termites.

NOT JUST FOR BIRDS

Platypuses and echidnas share a special bond. They are the only two mammals in the world that are monotremes. Monotremes are mammals that lay eggs.

Other mammals have been introduced to Australia. European settlers brought sheep and cattle to Australia. Sheep first arrived in 1788. Today, there are more than 150 million sheep in Australia. That's almost eight times as many sheep as people!

Europeans also brought rabbits and foxes to Australia. Unfortunately, these animals spread quickly and became pests. Over the years, they have destroyed land and killed many native animals.

Sheep

Birds Many unusual species of birds soar through the skies or cruise the land of Australia. The kookaburra and parakeet are Australian birds of flight. The emu and kiwi travel by foot.

The kookaburra is a large island bird living in Australia, Tasmania, and New Guinea. Its cry sounds like a human's laughter. Kookaburras catch prey and pound it up against trees. It is believed they do this to tenderize the meat.

Parrots are a family of birds that includes parakeets, lorikeets, cockatoos, and lovebirds. These colorful birds prefer warmer climates like those found in Australia. Parrots have two toes facing forward and two toes facing backward. This makes them the only birds able to pick up food and put it in their mouths with their feet.

The emu is the second-largest bird in the world. Emus can grow to a height of 6½ feet. These tall birds usually eat grass, berries, fruit, and insects. Although they can't fly, emus are fast runners. Their long legs and powerful feet help them move up to 30 mph.

WHAT TOPS THE EMU?

The largest bird in the world is the ostrich, which is also a flightless bird.

The kiwi is a funny-looking bird with a large round body, long beak, and no tail. Its wings are too small for flight. Female kiwis lay eggs that weigh about one-fifth of their own body weight. (Imagine a 125-pound woman having a 25-pound baby!) The male kiwi keeps the eggs warm until they hatch.

Kiwis

HUMAN KIWIS

People from the nearby island of New Zealand are nicknamed Kiwis. This is because these birds originally came from New Zealand.

Reptiles, Amphibians, Insects, Spiders, and Ocean Life A large number of reptiles, amphibians, and insects also call Australia home. The Great Barrier Reef is home to many different kinds of fish and other water life.

Frilled lizard

Frilled lizards, perenties, skinks, goannas, and thorny devils are a few types of lizards that slither across the Australian land. Water-holding frogs, Saurian crocodiles, taipan snakes, and leaf-tailed geckos enjoy the warm, humid rain forests along the coasts of Australia.

Funnel-web and jewel spiders crawl in the coastal areas of Australia. Termites build huge nests called *termite mounds* that can be 30 feet tall. Queen Alexandra's birdwing butterflies glide through the Australian skies. With a wingspan up to a foot wide, these butterflies are the largest in the world.

As an island country, Australia is surrounded by water creatures. Cleaner fish and butterfly fish swim in the ocean waters. Many types of starfish, including the crown-of-thorns starfish, make their way across the ocean floor. Other sea creatures, such as weedy sea dragons, kouras, sponges, and giant clams, thrive in the Australian waters.

Butterfly fish

Giant clam

Starfish

CHAPTER 3

Looking Back Australia's History

THE ABORIGINES

The first Australians were the Aborigines. Although Aboriginal folklore says that these people have always lived in Australia, scientists have a different explanation. They think that the Aborigines migrated from Southeast Asia more than 40,000 years ago. At that time, the level of the oceans was lower than it is now. That made it easier for the Aborigines to cross from Asia to Australia.

Body painting is an important part of traditional Aboriginal ceremonies.

The first Aborigines were hunter-gatherers. They hunted animals for food and gathered seeds, nuts, and other plant material to eat. The men hunted and made tools and weapons. The women gathered and prepared food and cared for the children.

The Aborigines made tools, weapons, and other items from natural materials. They carved wood into clubs, spears, and boomerangs. They also used sticks to dig up plants, kill snakes, and open termite mounds to get food. Stones were used to grind seeds and nuts. Food was stored in containers made from bark or woven from grass. Clothes, medicine, shelter, and jewelry were also made from woods, stones, and plants. Nothing was wasted.

A BIT OF BOOMERANG HUMOR

What do you call a boomerang that won't come back?

A stick

The Aborigines had a special way to create farmland called *firestick farming*. Fires were used to clear large areas so grass and other plants could grow. These plants provided food for the people and attracted kangaroos and other animals. These animals were then hunted by the Aborigines.

Aborigines lived in groups called *tribes*. Larger tribes lived in places where there were more **resources** to support them. In areas that did not have many resources, the tribes were smaller. Tribes sometimes traded with one another and gathered for exchange ceremonies. Each tribe spoke its own language. Before the Europeans arrived in Australia, there were more than 200 different Aborigine languages.

THE ARRIVAL OF THE BRITISH

In 1770, Captain James Cook arrived in Australia. This British explorer mapped large parts of the country and claimed it for England.

In 1788, the first settlers from England arrived in Australia. These settlers were **convicts**. In the past, England had sent convicts to their colonies in America.

Captain James Cook

However, these colonies sought freedom from British rule and became the United States. England then had to find a new place to send its convicts. England continued sending convicts to Australia until 1868.

Other settlers followed the convicts. These new settlers were free people who were looking for land for farming or raising cattle. Others came to Australia looking for gold to strike it rich.

NAME THAT COUNTRY

When Portuguese and Spanish explorers first found the large landmass in the Southern Hemisphere, they called it *Terra Australis Incognita*, meaning "Unknown South Land." Later, British explorer Matthew Flinders was the first to sail around the entire continent, proving it was one island. Shortly after that, it became known as Australia.

Tasmania was named for Abel Janszoon Tasman, a Dutch sea captain. Tasman was one of the first sailors to visit the island he called Van Diemen's Land. Later, it was renamed Tasmania in his honor.

A TERRIBLE CHANGE

The arrival of the British settlers was a disaster for the Aborigines. The Europeans took the Aborigines' land without paying for it. These early settlers thought the Aborigines were **inferior**. Huge numbers of Aborigines were killed by Europeans or died from diseases brought by the settlers, such as smallpox, measles, and pneumonia. Millions more were forced off their land and had to live on government **reservations**. Aborigines who worked for Europeans received little or no pay. Later, Aborigine children were taken away from their families and sent to European-style schools. Over time, the Aborigines' traditions and way of life were destroyed.

During the late 1960s, the Aborigines began fighting to regain ownership of their land. In 1967, they were finally recognized as Australian citizens and began to earn basic rights. However, the Aborigines continue to struggle for equality even today.

EXPLORING AUSTRALIA

As more British settlers arrived in Australia, the face of the country began to change. The land was divided into six colonies. Cities such as Adelaide, Melbourne, and Perth were built on Australia's coasts. Explorers began mapping the country. In 1860, Robert O'Hara Burke and William John Wills became the first Europeans to cross Australia from north to south. That same year, an expedition led by John McDouall Stuart was the first European effort to reach the center of the continent.

THE COMMONWEALTH

On January 1, 1901, the six British colonies in Australia joined to form the Commonwealth of Australia. The British king (or queen) became the head of the state. His or her interests are represented in Australia by an official called the *governor general*. Today, Australia still recognizes the British **monarch**, but it is a separate country with its own government. Australia has a Parliament that makes the laws. The Parliament is divided into the Senate and the House of Representatives. The prime minister is the head of the Australian government.

Australia's Old Parliament House in Canberra was the site of the national government from 1927 to 1988. It is now a museum that features the political, historical, and architectural heritage of the country. A new Parliament House was built in 1988.

CHAPTER 4

Digging In to Australia's Resources and Industries

Australia is a country with a stable **economy**. The many available **natural resources** support this strong system. Most of the country's wealth comes from farming and mining.

AGRICULTURE

Australia has a variety of agricultural resources. About two-thirds of the land in Australia is used for grazing or farming.

The dry grasslands in the outback are perfect for raising sheep and cattle. Sheep are raised in the southwest and southeast. Australia is the world's largest exporter of wool. Cattle are raised mainly in the drier areas of central and northern Australia. The country is a leading producer of beef. Half of the beef in Australia is exported, or shipped, to other countries.

Only about seven percent of the land is used for crop farming. Because the farms in Australia use high-tech equipment, this small number of farms is able to produce enough food for the whole country.

Wheat is the most important crop in Australia. It is grown on almost half of the land used for crops. Most wheat is grown in the southern part of Australia.

Sheep are often raised alongside fields of wheat. Areas where sheep herds and wheat fields are near one another are called *sheep-wheat belts*.

Other crops grown in southern and eastern Australia are oats, barley, rye, hay, rice, and cotton. Fruits such as oranges, apples, bananas, pears, peaches, and pineapples are common along the more tropical coasts. Several parts of Australia support grape vineyards. The grapes are then used to make wine.

Sheep shearing is big business in Australia. Shearers work in teams and often clip up to 500 sheep a day. They must be careful to remove the fleece in one piece.

Australia exports more than 75 percent of its wheat crop.

MINERALS

Australia is rich in mineral resources. The mining industry makes up about 25 percent of the country's economy. Bauxite, coal, diamonds, gold, iron ore, natural gas, nickel, petroleum, and uranium are abundant in the country.

Australia is the world's largest producer of bauxite. This mineral is the main source of aluminum.

Australia's coal production is used to make electricity for the country's homes and businesses. Coal mines are found in New South Wales, Queensland, and Victoria.

Australia is the world's largest producer of diamonds. About 40 percent of the world's diamonds come from Australia. A huge mine, the Argyle Diamond Mine, is located in Western Australia.

Gold was discovered in Australia during the 1850s. This discovery led to a huge wave of new settlers who were eager to make their fortunes. Today, Australia produces about 13 percent of the world's gold. Most of this gold is found in Western Australia.

Western Australia also produces about 95 percent of the country's iron ore. Other iron ore **reserves** are found in South Australia, Tasmania, and Victoria. Almost all of the iron ore is exported to other countries, including Japan, China, Germany, and South Korea.

Petroleum and natural gas are two other important resources in Australia. Millions of barrels of petroleum are produced from reserves in Western Australia, Queensland, and **offshore** areas. Australia's natural gas is used to produce heat and light energy for the country.

Areas of Australia have huge **deposits** of uranium. Uranium mines are located in the Northern Territory and South Australia.

OH, THOSE OPALS!

Australia is the opal capital of the world. The country produces 95 percent of all precious opals. Black opals can only be found in Lightning Ridge, New South Wales.

An opal is a gemstone that changes color as light reflects, or bounces, off it. Black opals have a black background color but still reflect the colors of light.

WATER

Water is an important resource for people and animals. Although Australia has only a few freshwater rivers, many artesian springs sit deep beneath the ground. An artesian spring is water trapped under so much pressure that when it finds a pathway, it gushes to the surface of the earth. Artesian water can be used just by digging a well. It does not have to be pumped.

The largest source of artesian water is the Great Artesian Basin, which covers almost a fourth of the continent. This basin stretches across most of eastern Australia.

Most of the water in the Great Artesian Basin, as well as other basins in Australia, is too salty for humans to drink. Livestock, however, are able to drink this water. In recent years, technology has made it possible for humans to **purify** this water source to provide for Australia's growing population.

TOURISM

One of the fastest growing areas of Australia's economy is tourism. Some people choose to test their strength and wit by trekking through the outback. Others prefer the adventures that Australian city life has to offer.

Along with the country's beautiful scenery, tourists enjoy attractions such as zoos, art galleries, museums, historic sites, and national parks. Some of the most popular attractions are the Great Barrier Reef, Ayers Rock, Kakadu National Park, the Sydney Opera House, and the many beautiful beaches in Sydney, Brisbane, and other coastal cities.

In 2000, Sydney hosted the Summer Olympics. This was the second time Australia held the Olympic Games. Melbourne was the host of the Summer Games in 1956. The 2000 event brought even more tourists to the country and showed the world what an exciting and beautiful place Australia is.

A BUNCH OF BEACHES

Looking for a place to enjoy some fun in the sun? Try one (or more) of Australia's beaches. With 7000 beaches, Australia has more sandy fun than any other country in the world.

Sydney Harbor

CHAPTER 5

The Many Faces of Australia

Discovering Australia's People

IMMIGRANTS AND NATIVES

About 95 percent of the people who live in Australia have a European background. Most of these people have roots in England or Ireland. Some are **descendants** of the settlers who began arriving in the 18th century. Others have come more recently to start a new life in Australia.

People have also emigrated, or moved, to Australia from other countries. Australia's population includes people from Hong Kong, China, Taiwan, Vietnam, and Indonesia.

Australia's native people, the Aborigines, still have a strong presence in the country. Most Aborigines live in **rural** areas, but increasing numbers have moved into **urban** settings.

WHO OR WHAT IS AN AUSSIE?

An Aussie is a person who originally lived or now lives in Australia.

LIFE IN THE OUTBACK

Life in the Australian outback can be harsh and difficult. Many of these "bush dwellers" live on isolated ranches or sheep stations. Because they are so far from schools, hospitals, stores, and other public places, the Australian government has made special services available to people who live in the outback.

The School of the Air uses two-way radios to teach children who live in remote areas. The first of these schools began in the town of Alice Springs in 1951. Today, about 1000 students are enrolled in 12 different schools. The two-way radios link teachers with students in the outback. The students can use the radios to ask questions and take part in classroom activities. Lessons are exchanged by mail every two weeks. In addition, teachers travel through the outback to meet their students. Minischools and camps are also held to bring students together.

The Flying Doctor Service uses small airplanes to bring medical help and supplies to bush dwellers. The Flying Doctor Service was founded in 1928 by a minister named John Flynn. Today, Australia has 14 Flying Doctor centers.

LIFE IN THE CITIES

Because of the harsh conditions in the outback, most of Australia's population live in the cities along the coast. Many people live in small houses with gardens and pools. Others live in apartments called *flats*.

CAN YOU NAME THE CAPITAL CITIES?

Each state in Australia has a capital city. Luckily for them, Australian students only have six capitals to memorize.

State	Capital
Western Australia	Perth
Queensland	Brisbane
South Australia	Adelaide
New South Wales	Sydney
Victoria	Melbourne
Tasmania	Hobart

Skyscrapers in downtown Sydney

People who live in Australia's cities and suburbs have similar lifestyles to people who live in the United States or Western Europe. They wear modern clothes, go to updated schools, and enjoy leisure activities, such as sports, movies, and concerts. Because Australia has a warm climate, outdoor activities are also very popular. Favorite pastimes include picnics, swimming, surfing, sailing, biking, Australian football, and a British sport called *cricket*.

Cricket is a sport in which players use a bat to try to "bowl" the ball through the opponent's wicket.

FAMOUS FACES FROM AUSTRALIA

Australia has a fascinating list of people who have made important contributions to the history of the country. Captain James Cook was the first to claim Australia for Britain. Arthur Phillip brought the first British settlers to the island. Edward Eyre, Hamilton Hume, William Hovell, and Charles Sturt explored the land and waters of Australia. Abel Janszoon Tasman discovered Tasmania. George Bass and Matthew Flinders sailed around Tasmania, proving it was a separate island.

Flinders then sailed around the entire continent of Australia. Edmund Barton became the first prime minister of Australia in 1901.

Many Australians have also gained worldwide fame. They have made great accomplishments in music, sports, and entertainment. Contemporary musicians from Australia include Savage Garden, Silverchair, Nick Cave, and Natalie Imbruglia. The Bee Gees, Air Supply, INXS, AC/DC, Men at Work, and Olivia Newton John are other Australian musicians.

Sports lovers may recognize the names of Cathy Freeman, Dawn Fraser, Greg Norman, Ian Thorpe, and Mick Doohan. Evonne Goolagong Crawley was the first Aborigine to win the Wimbledon Tennis Tournament.

The entertainment world would not be the same without talented Australians such as Mel Gibson, Nicole Kidman, Hugh Jackman, Russell Crowe, Geoffrey Rush, Cate Blanchett, and Paul Hogan (Crocodile Dundee). Movie giants Judy Davis and Errol Flynn were also from Australia.

PRIZE FOR PENICILLIN

Have you ever taken penicillin to help you feel better when you're sick? If so, you can thank Australian Howard Walter Florey. His work with penicillin enabled humans to use the drug to treat bacterial infections. Florey won a Nobel Prize for his accomplishments.

Evonne Goolagong (right) and Chris Evert Lloyd (left) at the 1980 Wimbledon Championships

Mel Gibson in the motion picture *Braveheart*

CHAPTER 6

A Slice of Life

Australian Culture

LANGUAGE

"G'day, mate, welcome to Oz." Do you know what that means? It means "Hello, friend, welcome to Australia."

Australians speak English. However, they still use some British words, such as *biscuit* for cookie or cracker, *lift* for elevator, and *tap* for faucet. The Aborigines and other native Australians also added words to the Aussie language. This blend of languages has created a unique sound only heard in Australia.

A LESSON IN AUSSIE LANGUAGE

Australian Term	English Translation
barbie	barbecue grill
bickies	money
bloke	man
dummyspit	temper tantrum
fair dinkum	honest
footy	Australian football
good on ya	well done; approval
jumbuck	sheep
lollies	candy
ripper	terrific
Sheila	woman

FOOD

Australians eat the same types of food that Americans do. However, there are some things on an Australian menu that may seem unusual. For example, many Australians eat kangaroo. Vegemite is a black yeast spread that many Aussies enjoy. Because of the abundance of sheep, lamb dishes are very common "down under." Australians also eat British foods, such as fish and chips (fried fish and french fries), shepherd's pie (a mixture of chopped meat and vegetables in a mashed-potato crust), and trifle (a layered dessert made of sponge cake and fruit).

Traditional Australian shepherd's pie is made with lamb. The dish got its name from the shepherds who herded flocks of grazing sheep.

PREPARING PAVLOVA

Pavlova is one of Australia's delicious desserts. It is named after Anna Pavlova, a famous ballerina.

ingredients

4 egg whites

a pinch of salt

1 cup granulated sugar

1½ teaspoons cornstarch

1 teaspoon vanilla

1 teaspoon vinegar

whipped cream

sliced fruit (strawberries, kiwis, peaches, etc.)

directions

1. Preheat the oven to 300°F.
2. Use an electric mixer to beat the egg whites and salt on high speed. Add the sugar a little bit at a time. Keep beating the mixture until it is very stiff.
3. Add the cornstarch, vanilla, and vinegar to the egg mixture. Stir until mixed.
4. Spoon the batter into a greased aluminum pie plate or a baking dish lined with greased aluminum foil. Press the batter down in the middle so the edges are a bit higher.
5. Bake for one hour at 300°F. Turn the oven down to 210°F. Bake for another hour.
6. Turn the oven off and open the door. Leave the baked shell in the oven until it's cool.
7. Remove the shell from the oven, and place on a serving plate. Fill the middle with whipped cream. Place sliced fruit around the edges. Cut and serve!

SPORTS

Outdoor sports are especially popular in Australia. Tennis, fishing, beach volleyball, swimming, and car racing top the list.

The most common team sports in the country are cricket, rugby, soccer, and Australian rules football. Cricket is a summer sport played with a bat and ball. Rugby is a form of football first played in England. Australian rules football was invented in Australia. It is only played there and on the nearby island of Papua New Guinea.

Australia is also home to the Melbourne Cup. This horse race is watched around the world.

HOLIDAYS

Christmas and New Year's Day are important holidays in Australia. Because these holidays occur during the summer in Australia, families are likely to celebrate with a picnic, a barbecue, or a day at the beach.

In addition, Australians celebrate Boxing Day on December 26. Boxing Day originated in England. Traditionally it is a day when gifts are given to service providers, such as mail carriers or garbage collectors.

Australians also celebrate several national holidays. January 26 of each year is Australia Day. On this day, the country remembers the day Arthur Phillip established the first British colony on Australia. His settlement later became the city of Sydney.

BOX IT UP!

Where did Boxing Day get its name? Years ago in England, servants were expected to work on Christmas Day to help the wealthy people with their holiday preparations, meals, cleanup, etc. The servants were then given December 26 off to celebrate with their family and friends. They were given boxes full of gifts and food by their employers to thank them for their help.

Another important day in Australia is April 25. This is Anzac Day. Anzac Day honors a special group of soldiers called the **A**ustralia and **N**ew **Z**ealand **A**rmy **C**orps. These men fought with the British in World War I. They were known for their outstanding courage.

THE ARTS

Australia has a rich performing arts culture. A government organization called the Australia Council provides financial support to many opera and dance companies, theater groups, orchestras, artists, and writers.

The most famous performing arts center in Australia is the Sydney Opera House. This building opened in 1973. Today, it is the busiest performing arts center in the world. The Sydney Opera House has 1000 rooms, including five auditoriums, four restaurants, numerous studios, several libraries, and more. The building covers 4.5 acres and took 14 years to build. Its unusual shell design has made it one of the most recognizable structures in the world.

Sydney Opera House

Art has always been a common way for Australians to express themselves. The ancient Aborigines used natural materials to create paintings on rocks and tree bark. Today, Aboriginal works have become well-known in Australia and Europe. In addition, other painters, such as George Russell Drysdale and Frederick Ronald Williams, are recognized for their paintings of the outback and other Australian landscapes. Another famous artist is Sidney Nolan. He uses Australian history as a theme in his work.

Music is also an important part of Australian life. In general, Australian music is similar to music in the United States and Western Europe. Aussies enjoy a variety of music styles—pop, rock, country, etc. Rap music, however, is not common in Australia. In addition, local Australian music has its own unique sound.

SING A SONG OF AUSTRALIA

"Waltzing Matilda" is a well-known song from Australia. It is often sung at sporting and school events in the country. In America, waltzing is a type of gliding walk or dance. In Australia, it means to wander around.

The song is based on a legend about a man who was caught in the outback eating a stolen sheep. To avoid being arrested, the man jumped into a river and drowned. The legend says that the man's ghost still walks around the outback today.

The Aborigines have a long tradition of creating music. One instrument they use is called the *didgeridoo*. Didgeridoos are made out of wood from a eucalyptus tree that has been hollowed out by termites. Each instrument is four to six feet long. Beeswax is used to make a mouthpiece. Aborigines use circular breathing to play the didgeridoo. When circular breathing, a person breathes in through the nose and out through the mouth at the same time.

The Aborigines play traditional didgeridoos for entertainment, ceremonial rituals, meditation, and healing.

TRY THIS AUSTRALIAN TRIVIA

What animated movie about a pig was made in Australia?

Babe

What two children's TV shows come from Australia?

The Wiggles and *Bananas in Pajamas*

What futuristic science fiction movies starring Keanu Reeves were made in Australia?

The Matrix, *The Matrix Reloaded*, and *The Matrix Revolutions*

Babe **is a movie about a pig who learns how to herd sheep on an Australian sheep farm.**

CHAPTER 7

What's Ahead?

A Look at Australia's Future

Australia has seen both positive and negative changes in recent years. Today, the country is still showing strong growth, but some challenges remain.

THE ABORIGINES

One of the most important and difficult issues in Australia is the treatment of the Aborigines. Over the past 35 years, Aborigines have gained rights such as the right to vote. Some land has been returned to the Aborigines. Others who lost their land to British settlers have received payment.

Despite the improvement in their legal position, Aborigines still struggle to find equality. Most of them continue to live in poverty. They suffer from a high rate of unemployment, a lack of health care, inadequate housing, poor schools, racial discrimination, and the loss of their native traditions.

GOING FOR THE GOLD

Cathy Freeman is an outstanding athlete who has won many track honors. She has also helped to make the world aware of the poor treatment of Aborigines in Australia.

In 1994, Freeman won the 200-meter race at the Commonwealth Games. During her victory laps, she carried both the Australian and Aboriginal flags.

Freeman was chosen to light the torch at the 2000 Olympic Games in Sydney. She also took home the gold in the 400-meter race. This made her the first Aborigine to win a gold medal in an individual event.

THE ECONOMY

Australia also faces economic challenges. Prices for mineral resources haven't been as stable lately as in the past. Poor growing seasons and difficulties finding good grazing land for sheep and cattle have created problems for farmers. Many towns in the outback are in danger of disappearing because their residents have moved to cities to find work and a better way of life.

Approximately four million people live in the busy city of Sydney.

THE ENVIRONMENT

Protecting the environment has also become important to Australians. Certain animal and plant species have become **extinct** because people have changed or destroyed habitats. Some places in the outback have turned into desert because of poor soil use and low rainfall.

Recently, the Australian National Parks and Wildlife Service set up a program called Save the Bush. This program aims to protect natural habitats. Meanwhile, the government is also educating people about caring for the land. A program called Greening Australia has planted more than one billion trees in an effort to increase resources and soil quality.

LOOKING FORWARD

Australia's people have always met challenges as they struggled to build a home on this unusual continent. Whatever the future holds, Australia will confront its problems with the same pioneer spirit that still lives in the hearts of its people.

Formed from sedimentary and volcanic rock, the MacDonnell Ranges of Australia are some of the world's oldest mountain ranges.

INTERNET CONNECTIONS AND RELATED READING FOR AUSTRALIA

Just the Facts!

http://www.gigglepotz.com/caustralia.htm
This "Kids Down Under" site is a great place to learn a little bit about everything Australian. It includes information, stories, maps, coloring sheets, quizzes, recipes, and more.

http://www.factmonster.com/ce6/world/A0805376.html
Let the "Fact Monster" teach you about the land, people, economy, government, and history of Australia.

http://www.nationalgeographic.com/resources/ngo/maps/view/images/australm.jpg
Take a look at Australia from space with this map highlighting many features of the country.

Chapter 1

http://www.kdu.com/ausform.html
Check out this easy-to-read summary of how the continent/country of Australia was formed.

http://www.australia.com/places_to_go/uw_unique_wonders/Prod_Map_STD1.aust?L=en&C=US
See the unique wonders that Australia has to offer, both geographic (Ayers Rock, Great Barrier Reef, Bungle Bungle, etc.) and human-made (Sydney Opera House and Sydney Harbour Bridge).

Chapter 2

http://www.dpiwe.tas.gov.au/inter.nsf/ThemeNodes/SJON-52B3JS?open
Explore nature in Tasmania by clicking on "wildlife" or "plants" for details on many of the island's unique species.

http://zoomschool.com/coloring/Australia.shtml
Find out more about the animals of Australia with the diagrams and information presented here.

Chapter 3

http://library.thinkquest.org/28994/index.html
The "History" section of this site will introduce you to the history of the Aborigines, the modern history of Australia, the Australian government, and a timeline of important events.

http://www.pbs.org/wnet/australia/
Use the "Interactive Timeline" at this site to put Australia's history in order.

http://www.factmonster.com/spot/aboriginal1.html
Find out more about the Aborigines with this easy-to-read information.

Chapter 4

http://www.reflections.com.au/MiningandExploration/Commodities/index.html
This site provides a brief overview of Australia's mineral wealth and links to information on various minerals.

http://mla.com.au/uploads/templates/otherpdf/MLA_Sheep_Sheet_2.pdf
What kind of sheep are raised in Australia? Check out the facts, charts, graphs, and map at this site to find out all about sheep farming in the country.

Chapter 5

http://www.australia.com/places_to_go/RHS_Top_STD.aust?L=en&C=US
Tour the many "places to go" in the cities and outback of Australia. Click on "outback," "farms & outback stations," and "cities" to learn about the different lifestyles and environments.

http://www.questacon.edu.au/html/school_of_the_air.html
What would it be like to go to school through the radio? Find out with this overview and history of the School of the Air.

http://www.rfds.org.au/history.htm
To learn more about John Flynn and the Flying Doctor Service he established, visit this official site of the Royal Flying Doctor Service of Australia.

Chapter 6

http://www.australiaday.com.au/big_events.html
This Australia Day Council Web site will teach you everything you want to know (and more!) about this national holiday. Check out the "Kids' Corner" for fun activities.

http://www.recipesource.com/ethnic/asia/australian/
From Anzac biscuits to kangaroo kabobs, these recipes will teach you how to cook (and eat) like an Aussie.

http://www.anzac.com/aust/nsw/soh.htm
Tour the Sydney Opera House through the facts, figures, and photos found here.

http://library.thinkquest.org/28994/music.html
This musical site provides more information on Australian music, the didgeridoo, and "Waltzing Matilda."

Chapter 7

http://www.smh.com.au
Catch up on Australian current events with *The Sydney Morning Herald* online.

Animal Geography: Australia by Joanne Mattern. Australia is a unique continent set apart from the rest of the world. The animals that inhabit Australia are just as unique. Perfection Learning Corporation, 2001. [RL 4.9 IL 4–9] (3141701 PB 3141702 CC)

Australia ABCs: A Book About the People and Places of Australia by Sarah Heiman. This book is an alphabetical exploration of the people, geography, animals, plants, history, and culture of Australia. Includes a traceable map and flag, locator map, symbols, and activity. Picture Window Books, 2003. [RL 3.8 IL K–4] (3432006 HB)

Crazy Creatures of Australia and New Zealand by Joanne Mattern. Read about some of the craziest creatures in the world found in Australia and New Zealand. Perfection Learning Corporation, 2001. [RL 3.9 IL 2–6] (3197301 PB 3197302 CC)

•RL = Reading Level
•IL = Interest Level
Perfection Learning's catalog numbers are included for your ordering convenience. PB indicates paperback. CC indicates Cover Craft. HB indicates hardback.

GLOSSARY

algae (AL jee) organisms, or living things, that grow underwater and float beneath or on the water's surface

British Commonwealth (BRIT ish CAH muhn welth) group of self-governing countries associated with a common loyalty to Great Britain (England)

brush (bruhsh) land covered with scrub plants (see separate entry for *scrub*)

convict (CAHN vikt) person who has been found guilty of committing a crime

deposit (dee PAHZ it) amount of a natural material, such as coal or oil, found in an area

descendant (dee SEN dent) relative who came after others

economy (ee CAH nuh mee) system of production, distribution, and use of goods and services in a country

elevation (el uh VAY shun) height above sea level

evergreen (EV er green) having leaves or needles that stay green year-round

extinct (EK stinkt) died out; gone forever

gorge (gorj) deep valley with steep sides

inferior (in FEAR ee er) less important than others; not as good

migrating (MEYE gray ting) traveling from one area to another

monarch (MAHN ark) person who rules a country; king or queen

native (NAY tiv) originally living or growing in a place

natural resource (NATCH er uhl REE sors) material found in nature

offshore (AWF shor) located in the waters near a shore

Parliament (PAR luh muhnt) legislative (lawmaking) body

plain (playn) area of flat, treeless land

plateau (plat OH) large raised area of land with a flat surface

purify (PYOOR uh feye) to remove material, such as salt from water, to make something clean or pure

reservation (rez er VAY shun) land set aside by the government for a special purpose, such as for groups of people being removed from other lands

reserve (RIZ erv) amount set aside for future use; supply

resource (REE sors) material that is valuable or useful, such as food, water, land, minerals, etc.

river system (RIV er SIS tuhm) river and all of the smaller bodies of water that flow into it

rural (ROOR uhl) having to do with life in the country

scrub (skruhb) type of plant with stunted or inferior growth (see separate entry for *stunted*)

stunted (STUHN ted) having short or poor-quality growth

territory (TAIR uh tor ee) area in a country that has some self-government but is largely controlled by a central government

tributary (TRIB you tair ee) stream or river that flows into another stream or river

urban (ER ben) having to do with life in the city

warm-blooded (warm BLUH ded) having a stable body temperature not dependent on the environment

INDEX